THE REVERSE
I CHING
(EAST)

and/or

"the book of reverse easy"

by:

The Hopi Book Club

EAST   8

SOUTH   28

WEST   48

NORTH   68

"Soul and body react sympathetically upon each other; a change in the state of the soul produces a change in the shape of the body and conversely, a change in the shape of the body produces a change in the state of soul"

-Aristotle

EAST

"We don't know"

We Don't Know

Togetherness

What is Not There

The Power of Compassion

The Humility of Power

Power of Penny

Depth and Compassion

We Don't Know

**Why ask
When you know it can't be answered?**

**Why write
When you know it can't be written?**

Therefore

The ancients say

"They who speak do not know "

- Tao Te Ching

Togetherness

**Sky no top
Abyss no bottom**

Therefore

The ancients say

"High and low arise together"

- Tao Te Ching

What is Not There

Split an atom
Enough to destroy world

Understand atom
Enough to save world

Therefore

The ancients say

"Power from what is not there"

- Tao Te Ching

The Power of Compassion

"Power is power
Whatever form it takes"

Therefore

The ancients say

"The old that is strong does not wither"

- J.R. Tolkien

The Humility of Power

Higher Power
Lower power
Great Power

Maybe they not in charge

Therefore

The ancients say

"It nourish all; yet take no credit
It is very small and has no aim"

- Tao Te Ching

Power of Penny

**Humble only to $100
Lack**

**Humble only to penny
Never lack**

Therefore

The ancients say

**"She who knows enough is enough
Will always have enough"**

- Tao Te Ching

Depth and Compassion

Three pigs in straw hut
Three pigs in rock hut

Deeper the compassion
Deeper the root

Therefore

The ancients say

"Deep roots are not reached
by the frost"

- J. R. Tolkien

"The old that is strong does not wither"

SOUTH

"Are you able to do nothing?"

Same Difference

Simple Rules

Wisdom of Do Nothing

Self and Others

Not Old Not Young

Wisdom of Longevity

Paradox of Separation

Same Difference

Like the earth
Go too far west
End up east

Therefore

The ancients say

"Look for difference; all different
Look for sameness; all same"

- Chuang Tzu

Simple Rules

If saint see only divine
And fool see only fool

When they meet
What they see?

Therefore

The ancients say

"The less rules and
regulations
The less thieves and
robbers"

- Tao Te Ching

Wisdom of Do Nothing

If you got two medicine
to choose from
And they both no work
Which you pick?

What if they give you
Four that no work
Are you better off?

Therefore

The ancients say

"Are you able to do
nothing?"

-Tao Te Ching

Self and Others

**If higher power
Lower power**

**If first place
Also last place**

Therefore

The Ancients say

**"Without others
There is no self"**

- Chuang Tzu

Not Old Not Young

"You peak you age"

Therefore

"See old as not old
Young as not young"

Wisdom of Longevity

Ancient turtle

Come last in rat race

Therefore

The ancients say

"Too much success is not an advantage"

- Tao Te Ching

Paradox of separation

"Body does not exists inside three dimensional space

Mind does not exist outside of it"

Therefore

The ancients say

"Carrying body and soul
And embracing the one
Can you avoid separation?"

- Tao Te Ching

"Are you able to do nothing?"

WEST

"All that is gold does not glitter"

Ride the Reverse

Receiving

Fool's Luck

Money and Compassion

Wisdom of Penny

Movie and Compassion

Endurance

Ride the Reverse

You hit bottom

The more you content

The easier you rise

Therefore

"This is called double efficiency"

- Chuang Tzu

Receiving

**Before having
There is not having**

Therefore

The ancients say

"The wise empty their desires"

- Tao Te Ching

Fool's Luck

Luck is spontaneous
Luck is helpful
Luck attract luck

Therefore

The ancients say

"Childlike folly brings good fortune"

The I Ching

Money and Compassion

If money god was a person
She hang out with
compassion

If compassion was a dude
They be hanging out

Therefore

The ancients say

"All that is gold does not
glitter"

- J.R. Tolkien

60

Wisdom of Penny

A buck want to be $100
and when
Buck became $100
$100 became the buck

A buck want to be penny
And when
Buck became penny
Penny became the buck

Therefore

The ancients say

"Magnify the small"

- Tao Te Ching

Movie and Compassion

Camera project movie
Sun project light

If you inside a movie
You may think camera is the
Black hole or creator

Therefore

The ancients say

"There seems to be a director; yet we can find no trace"

- Chuang Tzu

Endurance

"From where the sun now stands
I shall fight no more forever"
- Chief Joseph 1877

The sun moved
Not the Chief

Therefore

The ancients says

"He who stays where he is endures"

-Tao Te Ching"

"Magnify the small"

NORTH

"Effective Communication"

Play Game

Effectiveness

Communication

Power of a Chicken

Laugh

Different Sameness

Power of Innocence

Play Game

Deep down

We all kids pretending to be adult

Playing with other kids
Who are also pretending to be adult

Play game too serious

Kid part forgotten

Mask won't come off

Therefore

"Go to war

Not violence"

Effectiveness

It is more effective

To impress the kid

Than the mask

It is more lasting

To relate to the kid

Than the mask

Therefore

"Know the mask as mask
the kid as kid"

Communication

If you use mask to talk to a mask : The mask will use mask to talk to you

Use mask to talk to kid: Kid will use mask to talk to kid in you

Therefore

"See lion as kitten

Dragon as chicken"

Power of a Chicken

Crazy dragon humbling to
Mighty chicken

Mightier the chicken
Crazier the dragon

Therefore

The ancients say

"Power from what is not
there"

Tao Te Ching

Laugh

**Inward outward
All directions**

**If you can laugh both
ways
Laugh be you both ways**

Therefore

The ancients say

"Oh yes, I am a fool!"

- Tao Te Ching

Different Sameness

"Treat others as how you want to be treated"

Therefore

The ancients say

"Look for difference; all different
Look for sameness; all same"

- Chuang Tzu

Power of Innocence

We come from it
We return to it

Therefore

The ancients say

"To die but not to perish
is to be eternally
present"

- Tao Te Ching

"Power from what is not there"

www.ingramcontent.com/pod-product-compliance
Lightning Source LLC
Chambersburg PA
CBHW070326100426
42743CB00011B/2570